RESPONSIVE CLASSROOM

ENERGIZE

YOUR MEETINGS!

35

Interactive

Learning Structures

FOR Educators

All net proceeds from the sale of this book support the work of Northeast Foundation for Children, Inc. (NEFC). NEFC, a not-for-profit educational organization, is the developer of the *Responsive Classroom®* approach to teaching.

ISBN: 978-1-892989-62-8
Library of Congress Control Number: 2014937219

Cover and book design by Helen Merena
Cover photographs © Jeff Woodward. All rights reserved.
Interior silhouettes by Lynn Zimmerman

Northeast Foundation for Children, Inc.
85 Avenue A, P.O. Box 718
Turners Falls, MA 01376-0718

800-360-6332
www.responsiveclassroom.org

Printed on recycled paper

ACKNOWLEDGMENTS

As the developer of the *Responsive Classroom*® approach to teaching and the publisher of this book, Northeast Foundation for Children (NEFC) wishes to thank the many people whose hard work and dedication to children and educators have made this book possible. They include Ellen Shulman, school improvement specialist, Minneapolis Public Schools, Minnesota; Teri White, principal, Mary L. Fonseca Elementary School, Fall River, Massachusetts; *Responsive Classroom* consultant Karen Poplawski, who served as content advisor for this book; *Responsive Classroom* consultant Carol Davis; NEFC executive director Lora Hodges and directors Mary Beth Forton, Richard Henning, and Marc Swygert; NEFC senior editor/writer Jim Brissette, who served as project manager of this book; and the rest of the publications staff—Lynn Bechtel, Cathy Hess, Helen Merena, Elizabeth Nash, and Alice Yang.

CONTENTS

Energize Your Meetings!

Holding professional meetings at school is one of the most important ways to support staff in raising the quality of their instruction. School and district leaders across the nation work hard to guide staff through productive meetings, with meaningful content and the lively exchange of ideas.

Sometimes, though, our adult meetings fall short of being fully engaging and productive, becoming something to be tolerated rather than welcomed. The familiar lecture-style meeting, where the goal is to "get the information out and get it out quickly," can leave participants feeling disengaged and facilitators weary. How much learning occurs is an open question.

Just as our students need active and interactive classroom environments to do their best learning, so, too, do adults. They need to be actively engaged with their discussion leader, with one another, and with the content being covered. They need an environment that promotes risk-taking and honest, respectful dialogue.

In your hands, you hold a key resource that will help you make professional development (PD) sessions and staff meetings come alive with learning. From interesting ways to discuss an article to efficient techniques for airing opinions on an issue, the easy-to-use interactive structures in this book will get participants fully engaged. The result: more meaningful and productive gatherings, no matter the purpose or size of your group.

Already experienced at facilitating interactive meetings? You'll find plenty of ideas to add to your repertoire. Just beginning? This guide will get you off to a great start.

Tried and True

For more than three decades, facilitators of *Responsive Classroom*® workshops have been using these interactive structures to fully engage adult participants. Some structures were adapted from ones used successfully with children in the classroom; others were devised just for adults. Regardless, they have always been an essential element of *Responsive Classroom* workshops—and critical to their success.

These ideas for interactive learning allow professionals to engage with one another in dynamic but nonthreatening ways. Some structures, such as partners sharing thoughts on a question the group leader poses, are very simple. Others, such as small groups using a step-by-step approach to analyze possible solutions to a shared problem, are more involved. But every idea in this book will enable participants to work together effectively and strengthen their group intelligence while also building their individual knowledge.

Meeting a Wide Range of Goals

The thirty-five interactive learning structures in this book can help you reach a variety of meeting goals. For example, they can help your staff in:

> ➤ **Learning something new.** Suppose you're introducing a new way to teach a skill to students. You could open the meeting by using Mix and Mingle (page 34) to allow teachers to share with a series of partners what they already know about teaching this skill.

> ➤ **Deepening understanding of a topic.** When your team needs to go deeper with a topic, you can use Circle Map (page 14) to guide them in brainstorming ideas about the topic and then graphically categorizing and making sense of them.

> ➤ **Reflecting on learning and developing action steps.** If this is your goal, you could try Walk Around Survey (page 72) to help participants share key takeaways and ensure that everyone leaves the meeting with the same understanding.

➤ **Fully knowing procedures or protocols.** If you simply need to communicate information, such as new safety protocols, you can use Step-by-Step (page 60) to do so clearly yet interactively.

➤ **Solving a problem collaboratively.** Sometimes you need to bring a group together to discuss how to address a thorny issue, such as misbehavior in the cafeteria. Using a structure such as Narrowing Choices (page 38) ensures that all voices are heard, which can help the group better understand the problem and efficiently find a solution to try.

Besides thinking about your purpose for the meeting or PD session, consider your comfort level with using a particular structure, your knowledge of the group members, and their comfort level with trying new approaches to collaborative discussions and problem-solving.

Browse through the Learning Structures at a Glance (pages 6–7) to find ideas to try. You might want to start with a fairly straightforward one, such as Mix and Mingle (page 34) or Think, Pair, Share (page 64). Then, try another one for variety and to ensure that your sessions remain lively and your audience fully engaged.

THE FACILITATOR'S ROLE

Right after participants get started with their discussions in pairs or small groups, it's helpful if you make a quick tour around the room to assess whether everyone understood your directions and is getting to the task at hand. This way, you can clarify directions right away and, if needed, stop the whole group and clarify things for everyone.

Also, when circulating, try to be a "guide on the side" rather than the "sage on the stage." Listen in, nod, clarify misunderstandings, and gently redirect a group if it's off task, but avoid hovering too long or steering a conversation.

Of course, you may decide that it's important for you to participate directly, by talking one-on-one with a partner or as part of a small group. If so, still do the initial "drive-by" of all groups to make sure everyone is on track.

Tips for Success

➤ **Give clear instructions.** Summarize steps concisely or model them quickly. You could additionally show the steps on a chart. Alternatively, give out one step and have participants complete it before telling them the next step.

➤ **Point out potential challenges ahead of time.** For example, in Say Something (page 52), participants may be tempted to have a lengthy discussion about a point, rather than saying just one thing. Acknowledging such challenges up front can help participants anticipate them and stay on track.

➤ **Establish time limits.** You can project a visual timer from your computer to a screen (free timer apps are available) or simply give 1- or 5-minute warnings. This helps participants better manage their time and keeps the meeting moving along.

➤ **Avoid combining too many structures in one meeting.** It's helpful to have variety from meeting to meeting. But using many structures in one meeting can lead participants to focus on learning new structures instead of taking in the meeting content.

➤ **Have supplies ready.** Be sure pens, pencils, markers, paper, and handouts are ready to go. You may also want to have extra handouts available for unexpected participants.

➤ **Teach and use a signal for quiet attention.** Instead of repeatedly calling out "Time's up" or "Can I have your attention?" use a simple signal such as raising your hand or ringing a chime. Give the signal and then wait until everyone has stopped and focused on you.

➤ **Use quick, simple ways to form groups.** Counting off, grouping by grade level, or signing up on a chart can all work. You may also want to assign groups or pairs in advance to ensure participants work with a variety of people. In general, four to five people is the ideal size for a small group.

➤ **Set up a chart for burning questions.** To manage questions, write them on a chart as they come up (or have participants do this on their own). Address questions at the end of the meeting, save them for a later meeting, or send out a follow-up email with the questions and answers.

➤ **Give everyone a chance to speak.** The structures in this book provide opportunities for everyone to be heard, but one or more people can still sometimes dominate. Keep discussions inclusive by, for example, setting time limits for each speaker or limiting sharing to one comment per person. State explicitly that cross-talking or side conversations need to wait until everyone has had a chance to be heard.

LEARNING STRUCTURES AT A GLANCE

The descriptions below show a common use for each idea in this book. Once you and your group are familiar with an idea, you can adapt it for other purposes.

STRUCTURE	OFTEN USED FOR	PAGE
Brainstorming and Consolidating	Problem-solving and consolidating ideas into an action plan	**8**
Card Sort	Increasing understanding by examining various scenarios related to a specific topic and sorting them into categories	**10**
Carousel	Discussing various aspects of a topic while physically rotating from area to area	**12**
Circle Map	Brainstorming ideas and then making sense of them by using a graphic organizer	**14**
Closer Look	Previewing new information, such as new policies, in a relaxed format	**16**
Colored Dots	Contributing data on an issue and using that data to guide discussions or problem-solving	**18**
Commonalities	Finding commonalities in ideas on an issue and using them to guide a discussion about next steps	**20**
Geometric Forms	Reflecting on and wrapping up a presentation or workshop	**22**
Info Exchange	Finding inspiration through selected quotes	**24**
Inside-Outside Circles	Having quick one-on-one exchanges with many people	**26**
Jigsaws	Becoming "experts" on a topic and then sharing knowledge in small groups	**28**
Last Word	Having an in-depth consideration of text during small-group discussions	**30**
Maître d'	Exchanging ideas in a relaxed format with small groups of varying sizes	**32**
Mix and Mingle	Having multiple brief conversations to gather perspectives and build connections	**34**
Museum Walk	Exploring test or survey results, samples of students' work, or other information posted around the room	**36**

Brainstorming and Consolidating

IN BRIEF: Participants brainstorm ideas for solving a problem and then consolidate their ideas into categories that will help them formulate a practical action plan.

HOW TO DO IT

1 **Pose a "big question" that gets at the heart of the problem you're asking participants to address.** For example:

> "What can we do to make dismissal time calmer and friendlier for both adults and students so that the day ends on a positive note?"

2 **Remind participants of general guidelines for brainstorming:**

➤ The goal is to generate a list of ideas, not to evaluate or judge them. There are no right or wrong ideas.

➤ Everyone gets a chance to speak.

➤ Hold any comments or questions for later. One exception: Asking clarifying questions is OK.

➤ Silence is OK. Natural pauses allow participants to think of new ideas or be more willing to share them.

3 **Participants begin brainstorming responses to the big question** while you or a volunteer record their ideas on a chart or whiteboard. (Alternatively, have participants use sticky notes to write and post their ideas.) Allow no more than 10 minutes, which should be plenty of time to generate a list of ideas but not so much time that participants start to disengage.

CONTINUED

4 Guide participants as they sort the ideas into three to six broad categories. For the example question, categories might be:

➤ Expectations and Rules

➤ Teaching and Modeling Procedures

➤ Logistics

➤ Role of Adults

Allow about 10 minutes for this step.

5 **Participants form small groups.** Assign one category to each group. Groups discuss the ideas in their category and create a "solution statement" that encompasses those ideas. For example:

> "Children need to be retaught the rules and expectations for dismissal and to be reminded of them frequently in a positive, encouraging way. Teachers and other staff will take a minute or so to do this reminding as a regular part of their closing circle or end-of-day routines."

6 **Bring the groups back together** and share the solution statements.

Learning Structure in Action

Moving to Inquiry-Based Science Instruction

A teaching team has learned that they need to adopt an inquiry-based science instruction (IBSI) approach beginning next fall. To help prepare the school's science department staff for this change, the curriculum director and department head planned a series of staff meetings on the topic of IBSI.

For the first meeting, they used Brainstorming and Consolidating to generate ideas in response to this big question: "What do we

as a department need to do to ensure successful implementation of IBSI?"

After brainstorming, the staff sorted the ideas into four categories:

1. Curriculum Goals
2. Lesson Planning
3. Instruction
4. Assessment

Next, small groups created solution statements, which were then used as the focus for subsequent department meetings.

Card Sort

IN BRIEF: Participants reach a shared understanding of a topic—for example, what constitutes effective implementation of a teaching practice, such as scaffolding—by sorting scenarios into categories. For facilitators, a way to assess a group's understanding of a topic; can also be used for problem-solving.

HOW TO DO IT

1 **In advance, create the following:**

➤ **Scenarios related to the topic in question.** For example, if you want staff to reach a common understanding of scaffolding, you would come up with different scenarios of teachers scaffolding their teaching. Print the scenarios on index cards. You'll need enough for each small group of particpants to have three to five scenarios, though it's OK to repeat scenarios. (See sample scenarios on the next page.)

➤ **Categories of effectiveness** that the scenarios can be sorted into. For example, in the case of scaffolding, the categories might be *effective scaffolding*, *moderately effective scaffolding*, and *ineffective scaffolding*.

2 **Participants form small groups.** Give each group their scenarios to evaluate and sort into the categories you established. Allow 10 minutes or so for this step.

3 **Bring the whole group back together** and invite one small group to explain its evaluation of one scenario. Ask whether any group disagrees and, if so, why. Repeat as time allows.

Alternatively, each group can display its card sort, and everyone can walk around to look at and reflect on the different card sorts.

4 **Open a broader discussion of the topic** using the sorted scenarios as a prompt.

Sample Scenarios

> Before students begin writing essays, the teacher gives small groups of students model essays that reflect each rubric score.

> Before students begin reading a new chapter, the teacher gives them definitions of a few words that students may find especially challenging.

> Before students begin analyzing an article, the teacher decides not to have them use graphic organizers to try to save time.

Learning Structure in Action

Building a Shared Understanding of Differentiation

A school's instructional coach wants to ensure that everyone on staff has the same understanding of differentiation and how it should be implemented in the classroom. He decides to use Card Sort. The levels of implementation he comes up with are:

➤ **Fully** meets our definition of differentiation
➤ **Partially** meets our definition of differentiation
➤ **Does not** meet our definition of differentiation

The instructional coach then gives each group different classroom scenarios to evaluate and sort according to these levels. After the whole group has discussed a few scenarios for each level, he initiates a conversation about ways to implement differentiation consistently in every classroom, according to the school's common definition.

Carousel

IN BRIEF: Large sheets of chart paper representing subtopics within a main topic of discussion are posted around the room. Participants move from chart to chart discussing these subtopics and recording their ideas. Useful for exploring a topic in some depth in a short amount of time (and it gets participants up and moving).

HOW TO DO IT

1 **Post pieces of chart paper** (no more than six) throughout the room. Label each chart with one subtopic of your main topic. For example, if your main topic is chaotic cafeteria climate, the subtopics might be the key areas or times in the cafeteria when behavior breaks down.

2 **Introduce the activity.** For example:

> "We'll form small groups and move from chart to chart to discuss these key areas and times in the cafeteria when we've noticed students misbehaving."

Suggest that participants focus their discussions on certain specifics. In this case, they could focus on examples of misbehavior at each location or time and the likely causes of the misbehavior.

3 **Participants form one small group per chart.** A volunteer from each group serves as the group's scribe. Give a different-colored marker to each scribe.

4 **Each group takes 2 to 3 minutes to discuss their subtopic** while the scribe records ideas on the chart.

Cafeteria Issue #2 Returning Trays, Disposing of Trash	
Issue:	Possible Reason(s):
• Trays and trash left on tables.	• Students rushing to leave. • Procedures for exiting cafeteria not consistent among classes.

CONTINUED

5 On your signal, groups rotate clockwise to the next chart, read the previously recorded ideas, and add new ideas.

6 Continue until all groups have visited and contributed ideas to each chart. (You may also want to invite participants to quickly review the charts again to see all the ideas that have been added.)

7 Debrief as a whole group. Reflection questions can be about patterns noticed, further questions, or insights gained. You may also want to highlight ideas on the charts that most resonate with the group.

Learning Structure in Action

Building Literacy Skills in Social Studies

A teacher leader wants to help teachers reinforce Common Core literacy skills during the next social studies unit. He posts four charts with these titles for groups to discuss:

➤ Vocabulary connections

➤ Informational text structures to use

➤ Informational text comprehension skills to teach/review

➤ Expository writing skills to teach/review

He uses Carousel to lead a discussion about how these aspects of literacy can be taught and practiced in the upcoming social studies unit.

Circle Map

IN BRIEF: Participants use a simple graphic organizer to brainstorm and categorize ideas on a given topic. Especially useful for capturing different perspectives and synthesizing information.

HOW TO DO IT

1 **Participants form small groups.** Give each group a sheet of chart paper and a different-colored marker (blue for one group, red for another, and so on). Ask for a volunteer scribe for each group.

2 **Each group makes a large circle and writes the discussion topic in the center.** Sample topics: "Ways to effectively integrate the Common Core State Standards in specials" or "How to implement a new bullying prevention initiative."

3 **Each group brainstorms as their scribe records their ideas on the chart paper** (within the circle and without trying to organize the ideas). Allow 5 to 7 minutes for this brainstorming.

4 **Each group exchanges papers with a neighboring group and reviews that group's chart.** They categorize the items and make a key on the chart to explain their categories (for example, a star next to an item = community building, a triangle = working with parents, etc.). Allow about 5 minutes for this step.

5 **Groups trade papers back for the original groups to review.** After 5 minutes or so, bring the whole group together to share key observations, such as similarities and differences among the charts, or to discuss next steps.

➤ Before the whole-group discussion in Step 5, display all the completed charts. Invite participants to walk around and reflect on all of them, then launch the whole-group conversation.

Learning Structure in Action

Shifting to a Workshop Model

A school's leadership team has been guiding teachers in transitioning to using a consistent workshop model for language arts instruction in every grade. The team selected several articles that reflect their ideal workshop model.

They pass out an article to each small group of teachers and allow time for reading. They then use Circle Map to have teachers list ideas from their article for implementing the workshop model at their school. Next, the teachers categorize the ideas and discuss common elements.

The leadership team uses this discussion to start developing guidelines for teachers to use as they set up their language arts workshops.

Closer Look

IN BRIEF: Participants preview new information, such as updated policy manuals and new curriculum materials, and share feedback in a relaxed way.

HOW TO DO IT

1 **Give each participant the materials to be previewed.** Then introduce the activity. For example:

> "I've given you each a set of math manipulatives that we're purchasing for kindergarten and grades one, two, and three. Let's all take 5 minutes to explore these on our own. Then we'll come back together and discuss our discoveries, thoughts, and questions."

2 **If you want participants to explore specific aspects of the materials,** come up with some open-ended questions to guide them. For example:

➤ "How would you use these in your math lessons?"

➤ "In what ways might children use them besides for math?"

Display these or write them onto the note-taking sheet on page 81, make copies, and pass them out.

3 **Ask volunteers to share their responses** to the questions you posed in Step 2. Or they can discuss one thing they noticed, one idea they had for using the materials, or one question it raised for them. List people's responses.

➤ After everyone has had a chance to share at least once, generate new ideas and questions by giving the group a few more minutes to explore the materials. You may want to give them additional questions to consider in this second round.

➤ If time is a factor or supplies are limited, have participants work in pairs or small groups.

➤ Invite volunteers to model any ideas they have for using the materials that may be new to the group.

Learning Structure in Action

Reviewing the Parent-Guardian Volunteer Handbook

A school's ad hoc committee has worked with its PTO leadership board to create a draft of a parent-guardian volunteer handbook. At a staff meeting, the committee invites participants to take a Closer Look at the draft, notice what pops out for them, and think about how the final handbook might be useful to their teaching and students' learning. Committee members then prompt a discussion by asking questions such as the following:

➤ "What are some general things you noticed about the draft?"

➤ "How might this handbook affect current volunteer opportunities you've already established?"

➤ "How could this handbook foster new volunteering ideas?"

➤ "How might this handbook help facilitate a conversation with a volunteer if a challenging situation arises?"

Based on what participants noticed during their Closer Look and the discussion that followed, the committee and board finalize the handbook and distribute it to the staff.

Colored Dots

IN BRIEF: The group generates ideas for meeting a goal and then uses stickers to vote on the ideas that seem most promising. The results of the vote give the leader a quick set of data to guide discussion or problem-solving.

HOW TO DO IT

1 **Post three to five charts around the room before the meeting.** Have dot stickers available at each chart.

2 **Label each chart with a subgoal of the main goal.** For example, if the main goal is to improve the overall school climate, one chart might be about improving hallway climate, another about improving bus climate, and so on.

3 **Invite participants to add their ideas to each chart.** Allow 5 to 10 minutes for this step.

4 **Participants circulate and read the charts.** At each chart, they use three stickers to "vote" for the ideas they think are most important. They can use their three stickers in any combination to show how strongly they view an idea (from one sticker per idea to all three stickers for just one idea). Allow 5 to 10 minutes for this step.

5 **Bring the whole group back together.** Tally up the votes, and use the results to guide a larger discussion of meeting the stated goal and subgoals. (You may want to allow a few minutes for small-group reflections before opening up the whole-group discussion.)

Improving Our School Climate: HALLWAYS

Post rules and expectations in each classroom. • • •

Post rules and expectations in each hallway. •

Model/review procedures and expectations every Monday/after every holiday. • • • • • •

Change displays more often. • •

Add more adult monitors. • • •

Use more student monitors. • • • •

➤ After discussing the results in Step 5, give participants a new set of stickers (of a different color or style) and have them re-vote to see if perspectives have shifted and more discussion is needed.

➤ Rather than limiting participants to three stickers per chart, give each of them ten or fifteen stickers and have them vote however they like.

➤ Adapt this structure into a way to assess understanding. For example, participants can use different-colored dots to indicate their level of understanding (red = low; yellow = some; green = high).

Learning Structure in Action

Reducing Conflicts at Recess

Because the assistant principal has been noticing a high rate of referrals from recess, she shares data about recess referrals with staff at their next meeting. Then she posts these three charts:

➤ "How can we improve recess supervision?"

➤ "How can we improve play options (structured/unstructured) during recess?"

➤ "How can we improve the physical space, equipment, and time management for recess?"

The assistant principal invites staff to list their ideas on each chart and then use Colored Dots to vote on the ideas they think are most important. She uses the results to work with staff in planning short- and long-term changes to recess routines and supervision.

Commonalities

IN BRIEF: Participants discuss an issue with a partner or small group and look for commonalities, or areas of strong agreement, in their responses. These commonalities are then used to help participants focus on possible solutions or next steps.

HOW TO DO IT

1 **State the topic for participants to discuss.** For example:

> "At your table, take a few minutes to discuss the latest math assessment results. What conclusions can you draw from these results?"

2 **As they discuss the topic, participants write down any commonalities in their responses.** Allow about 3 minutes for this step.

3 **Pose a new related topic.** For example:

> "Can we draw similar conclusions from the language arts assessment results, and why or why not?"

Repeat Step 2.

4 **Ask for volunteers to share their commonalities** (or write them down on sticky notes and post them). Use the commonalities to guide a whole-group discussion in this or a future meeting.

➤ In Step 3, instead of posing a new question, use the same question you posed initially but have participants get up and Mix and Mingle (see page 34), discussing the question with different partners.

➤ For variety, or to cover a wider range of topics, prepare several slips of paper, each with a different question. Give one slip to each small group to discuss.

Learning Structure in Action

Glitches in Transitions and Coverage Duties

The administration team has been receiving feedback about staff not showing up on time to meet students after specials, lunch, and recess. In addition, the team is hearing that staff are frequently late to duty stations for lunch, recess, and arrival/dismissal.

To sort out why these problems are occurring and how best to address them, the administration team starts a staff meeting by doing Commonalities. They ask staff to work in small groups and find commonalities for each of these questions:

➤ "Why are we struggling with transitions from specials?"

➤ "What can we do to ensure smoother transitions from specials?"

➤ "Why are we struggling with supervision coverage at recess, lunch, and arrival/dismissal?"

➤ "What can we do as a school to ensure consistent supervision coverage at these times?"

After the groups share their commonalities for each question, the administration team leads a discussion to home in on the key reasons for these struggles and practical ways to solve them. As a result, the team creates new procedures for smoother transitions and consistent supervision coverage.

Geometric Forms

IN BRIEF: Participants use a form to reflect individually at the end of a discussion or presentation. Helps the discussion leader quickly assess the group's understanding.

HOW TO DO IT

1 **To wrap up a discussion or presentation, have participants do some reflection.** For example, after a presentation about using open-ended questions during instruction, you might say:

> "This wrap-up activity will help you make sense of today's learning. It will also give me a sense of what everyone thinks about using more open-ended questions, and I'll use this information at our next meeting."

2 **Pass out copies of the Geometric Forms handout** on page 80. Allow participants several minutes to complete the form. Consider telling participants to keep their forms anonymous.

3 **Collect everyone's paper** and use the information to set the agenda for your next meeting on this topic.

VARIATION

➤ Before collecting the papers, ask participants to share one item from their form with a partner or invite volunteers to share with the whole group.

Learning Structure in Action

Incorporating Authentic Assessment

A school's academic coaches are looking for ways to incorporate more authentic assessment into students' learning experiences. After discussing the topic at a staff meeting, they use Geometric Forms to wrap up their discussion and get a sense of teachers' understanding and plans for how to include more authentic assessments in their lesson plans. Here are examples of some of the teachers' responses:

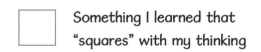 Something I learned that "squares" with my thinking

Students benefit from authentic assessments such as collaborating on real-world science investigations.

 A question that is still "circling" in my mind

How much planning time will be required to make all my assessments authentic?

 Three important "points" I want to remember

1) Use simple checklists and rubrics.

2) Work as a team to establish consistent criteria.

3) Use a variety of activities and structures.

 One new "direction" I will go in (or action I will take)

Collaborate more with my colleagues in our department to develop a common set of options for authentic assessments.

Info Exchange

IN BRIEF: This fun way of using selected quotes inspires staff to adopt a mindset that supports key goals for a department, school, or district.

HOW TO DO IT

1 **In advance, find quotes that are relevant to your goals.** For example, if your school is about to shift to a new curriculum, you might look for quotes from books and articles that help provide a rationale for this change.

2 **Print the quotes attractively on index cards or slips of paper.** You'll need one quote for each participant, but it's OK if quotes are repeated.

3 **Briefly introduce this activity.** For example:

> "We'll each get a card with a quote on it. We'll find partners and take turns sharing our quote and its significance, a connection we made to it, or a question it raises for us."

4 **Give each person a card and invite everyone to find a partner.** The partners discuss the quotes. If you want a focused discussion, provide a question for them to answer. For example:

> "How would you translate this quote into an action step for working with students?"

5 **Allow 3 to 4 minutes for discussion.** Then signal partners to swap their cards, find a new partner, and repeat the process for several more rounds, as time allows.

Learning Structure in Action

Creating a Culture of Success

A principal is determined to instill a positive tone and student-focused mindset for the whole school. She pulls quotes representative of a culture of school success from an inspiring book she read over the summer.

The principal then asks a student who has a good sense of graphic design to print out the quotes in an inspiring format, using the school colors and logo. At a staff meeting before the new school year starts, she uses Info Exchange to engage the staff and begin a conversation about cultivating a "culture of success" mindset.

Inside-Outside Circles

IN BRIEF: Participants have quick, one-on-one exchanges with many people in a short time. Handy for trading tips, short examples, or other information that doesn't require a lengthy discussion.

HOW TO DO IT

1 **Make sure the room is large enough to allow participants to form two concentric circles** with a comfortable talking space between them.

2 **Briefly introduce the structure.** For example:

> "We're going to form an inner and an outer circle to exchange ideas about how we might best use the new strategies that our instructional consultant shared with us."

3 **Participants count off by twos.** The ones form an inner circle, facing out, and the twos form an outer circle, facing in. Each two should be facing a one, forming a pair.

4 **State a question for discussion.** (Use questions that can be addressed fairly quickly.) Partners briefly exchange ideas. Allow about 1 minute for this.

5 **On your signal, the outside circle shifts one spot to the right** to form new pairs. The new partners discuss the same question, or a new question that you pose. Repeat as time allows.

6 **Bring the whole group back together for a quick debrief.**

➤ Depending on the size of the group and the shape of the meeting space, you can have participants form two sets of inside-outside circles.

➤ Use Inside-Outside Circles for skills practice. For example, describe a student misbehavior and have partners trade examples of clear, respectful redirecting language they can use to quickly restore positive behavior in that situation.

Learning Structure in Action

Improving Vocabulary Instruction

The literacy coach is facilitating a discussion about how to improve instruction for teaching vocabulary in light of the Common Core standards and their focus on text complexity. Using Inside-Outside Circles to warm teachers up for this bigger discussion, she has pairs briefly discuss the following questions:

➤ "How do you currently approach vocabulary instruction?"

➤ "How do you ensure vocabulary is appropriately challenging?"

➤ "How do you find texts that are appropriately challenging?"

After pairs discuss the first question, the literacy coach rings the signal chime. The outer circle shifts, new pairs discuss the next question, and so on. After 5 minutes, the group completes this Inside-Outside Circle warm-up and moves into their larger discussion.

Jigsaws

IN BRIEF: Participants read different selections of text, become "experts" on their selection, and then discuss the readings in small groups. Useful for exploring a book, major report, or series of articles. Dividing the reading reduces the load while still ensuring that everyone learns all main ideas and key details.

HOW TO DO IT

1 **Assign the readings in advance (if more than two or three pages)** or pass out copies for participants to read in the meeting.

2 **Divide participants into group of no more than five.** Assign each group a different reading, and give each person a copy.

3 **Introduce the activity.** For example:

> "As part of our ongoing discussion on positive discipline, I have four short articles for us to read. You'll each read just one article and then discuss it twice, first with others who've read it and then with those who haven't."

4 **Each small group discusses their reading and agrees on its key ideas.** Allow 7 to 10 minutes for this step.

5 **Members of each group count off.** All the ones from the various groups form a jigsaw group, all the twos another, and so on. Thus, each jigsaw group now has one member who can speak on each reading.

6 **In the jigsaw groups, each person shares the key ideas from their reading** and takes questions and comments.

Learning Structure in Action

Consistency in Addressing Common Behavior Issues

After collecting data, a principal identifies four common behavior issues to address. Using a recently published book on positive behavior strategies, she selects four chapters related to these behavior issues and assigns them to staff to read before their next meeting.

At the meeting, she uses the Jigsaw format. Staff synthesize key strategies from the four chapters and do the groundwork for developing a consistent schoolwide approach for addressing each behavior.

Last Word

IN BRIEF: A small-group activity that promotes a deeper understanding of a short piece of text (one to three pages long). For facilitators, a way to get a sense of what participants find important and use that information to guide further discussion.

HOW TO DO IT

1 **Give participants a copy of the text to read.** Note the purpose for this reading and have participants highlight a few sentences or phrases they found significant or have questions about. (Alternatively, ask participants to read the text before the meeting.)

2 **Participants form small groups of three to five to discuss the reading.** One participant is the first speaker and begins by reading a sentence or phrase that they highlighted.

3 **The person to the speaker's left responds with a question or connection to the sentence/phrase.** Continue around the group so that everyone has a chance to respond. (Participants can pass if they wish.)

4 **After everyone in the group has had a chance to respond, the speaker has the "last word."** For example, the speaker can briefly explain why they highlighted that sentence/phrase, sum up what the group said, or add on to someone's idea.

5 **Repeat the process until everyone has had a chance to share at least one sentence or phrase they highlighted.** To keep things moving at a lively pace, suggest that each round of discussion be limited to 5 minutes or less.

Learning Structure in Action

Going Deeper With an Education Journal Article

A curriculum advisor wants to help staff address the speaking and listening standards of the Common Core throughout the curriculum, particularly in math and science instruction. During the summer, he found a series of articles on this topic and plans to share them with staff throughout the school year.

He hopes the articles will build staff expertise in helping students become proficient in:

➤ Explaining the thinking they used to solve a math problem

➤ Summarizing the results of a science experiment

➤ Asking purposeful and respectful questions

➤ Answering questions thoughtfully, completely, and clearly

At various staff meetings during the year, he uses Last Word after the staff has read one of the articles to help them build on each other's understandings of how to teach students these essential speaking and listening skills.

Maître d'

IN BRIEF: Acting as a maître d', you call participants to "tables" of various sizes, where they "dine"— that is, exchange ideas—with a variety of tablemates. Especially useful when you want participants to share a wide range of ideas, rather than focus on a topic in depth.

HOW TO DO IT

1 **Introduce the activity.** For example, after discussing the importance of using reinforcing language, you might say:

> "I'm going to ask you to stand in small groups to share examples of reinforcing language you could use in a specific situation. Then I'll let you know when it's time to rearrange groups."

2 **Call out a number, such as "Table for three."** Participants quickly arrange themselves into groups of that number. (It's OK if some groups have one participant more or less. In general, limit each "table" to four or five participants.)

3 **Tell everyone what topic or question to discuss.** Let them know that to keep things moving and give everyone a chance to share, they'll have only a few minutes to talk. Give a 30-second warning before signaling each group change.

4 **Signal for the discussion to end.** Then repeat Steps 2 and 3 for two additional groupings.

Learning Structure in Action

Reviewing Schoolwide Math Assessment Data

The district's math teachers have previously seen and discussed schoolwide data, which indicate that students have high levels of competency in geometry, but low levels of number sense. The math curriculum coordinator plans a meeting and decides to use the Maître d' format to invite the math teachers to reflect on the data and begin to generate possible next steps.

He poses these questions to the group:

➤ Table for Three—"What shifts could you make in your whole-group instruction to boost students' number sense?"

➤ Table for Four—"What types of small-group learning can be used to lift this skill?"

➤ Table for Two—"What do you need to know about individual learners to better address this skill with them?"

After these discussions, the math teachers come away with some new strategies for improving students' number sense.

Mix and Mingle

IN BRIEF: Participants converse briefly and informally with different partners as they might during a casual social gathering. Especially useful as a warm-up activity and for introducing a new initiative or program and inviting participants' early thoughts on it.

HOW TO DO IT

1 **In advance, prepare three to five questions** that you want participants to discuss.

2 **Introduce the activity.** For example:

> "I'd like us to discuss three questions on working with children who are on the autism spectrum. I'll ask the first one, give you time to think, and then we'll each find a partner and discuss our thoughts on the question. After a few minutes, I'll ask another question. You'll mix and mingle to find a new partner to discuss that question with, and so on."

3 **Read or say aloud the first question for participants to consider.** Invite them to walk around the room for a minute while they think.

4 **Signal for them to find a partner and take turns discussing their thoughts.** Allow just a minute or two for this discussion.

5 **Repeat the mixing and mingling** with your remaining questions.

6 **Invite a few participants to share with the whole group** one key idea they discussed (either after each question round or after all the questions have been discussed).

VARIATION

➤ You may want to play some music as participants walk around thinking about the question you posed and looking for a chat partner. Also suggest that partners greet each other first, then talk about the question.

Learning Structure in Action

Using Literature Circles Consistently

Curriculum leaders want to ensure that a school's use of Literature Circles is consistent. They start a conversation about this relatively new initiative by inviting staff to participate in a Mix and Mingle activity, during which they discuss the following questions:

➤ "What is your understanding of why we use Literature Circles in our school?"

➤ "How do you currently teach students the steps for choosing an appropriate book for Literature Circles?"

➤ "What roles and responsibilities do you assign students for their book groups?"

➤ "What methods do you use to check students' understanding?"

➤ "How do you connect the relevant standards to students' work in their book groups?"

After the staff mix and mingle to discuss each question, the curriculum leaders bring everyone back together. As a whole group, the teachers generate a list of key ideas for setting up effective Literature Circles. This list serves as the starting point for developing a consistent approach for using this reading structure.

Museum Walk

IN BRIEF: Mimics a visit to a museum, but instead of looking at paintings or sculpture, participants walk around the room to view posted pieces of information on a teaching topic or technique, results from a test or survey, or student work samples. Especially useful for absorbing and interpreting a lot of data or complex information.

HOW TO DO IT

1 **Post displays of the information you want participants to absorb.** Spread the charts or displays around the room as you would pieces in a museum gallery.

2 **Briefly introduce the activity.** You may also want to pose a focused question or two for participants to think about on their walk. For example:

> "Take 10 minutes to walk around the room and study these charts that show math test results for each grade. As you walk, consider this question: 'What do these results tell us about the progression of math instruction from grade to grade?'"

3 **Invite participants to choose their own starting point for their walk.** Encourage them to partner up and talk with each other as they view the charts, and to take notes or put sticky notes on the displays with their comments and questions.

4 **Give participants a 5-minute warning and a 1-minute warning** so they know to wrap up their observations.

5 **Bring the group back together for a whole-group discussion** on what participants noticed and questions the information raised for them.

➤ Do a poster session and Museum Walk combination: Invite individual staff members or teams to create posters of strategies they've used successfully to meet a school goal. Display the posters and have the rest of the staff do a Museum Walk to view the posters and discuss them with the poster presenters.

Learning Structure in Action

Strengthening Writing Instruction

To help everyone develop a better understanding of the writing continuum—how students' writing progresses from one grade to the next—the literacy coach plans a staff meeting. Before the meeting, he asks every teacher to bring one strong student writing sample. He posts these samples around the room, with the grade identified but student and teacher names covered.

During their Museum Walk, staff study the samples and take notes, focusing on the common elements that make these pieces of writing strong. After bringing everyone back together, the literacy coach uses the following question to spark a lively discussion:

➤ "What do you notice about the progression of students' writings?"

After this discussion, he invites several volunteers to form a working group that will develop a set of grade-specific writing criteria and establish a writing continuum plan.

Narrowing Choices

IN BRIEF: Participants use a set of practical strategies to narrow down a long list of ideas for solving a problem.

HOW TO DO IT

1 **Brainstorm and list possible solutions to a problem.** Do this in advance of the meeting or as a whole-group activity at the start of the meeting.

2 **Working with partners or small groups, participants narrow the list** by using one or more of the following strategies:

➤ Plusses and Minuses—participants discuss the advantages and disadvantages of each idea.

➤ Unlivable Only—participants identify choices they *can't* live with and explain why.

➤ Livable Only—participants identify choices they *can* live with and explain why.

➤ Three Straws—participants name their top three choices and explain why.

➤ One Why—participants identify the one idea they prefer and explain why.

3 **Bring the whole group back together with their narrowed lists.** Ask participants to share their final thoughts on the problem and discuss which idea or set of ideas seems best to try first.

➤ Combine Narrowing Choices with Carousel (page 12): Post the brainstormed solutions on big sheets of paper around the room, one solution per sheet. Participants walk around as pairs or small groups and use one or more of the strategies under Step 2 to evaluate the solutions.

Learning Structure in Action

Improving the Climate in the Cafeteria

The assistant principal has become aware that many students are struggling to behave appropriately in the cafeteria. She starts planning how to provide the cafeteria duty teachers with effective strategies for respectfully and effectively addressing misbehavior.

Before meeting with the cafeteria duty teachers, she has them read a brief packet of information about promoting positive behaviors in the cafeteria and other common areas. Then, at the meeting, they brainstorm a list of strategies they think might work (based on the readings) and use Narrowing Choices to decide on three strategies to try for the next few weeks before reassessing at a future meeting.

One-Sentence Summary

IN BRIEF: Participants sum up their learning by making one brief statement. For facilitators, useful for checking to see what key points participants learned and gauging how well those points were communicated.

HOW TO DO IT

1 **Invite participants to reflect on a presentation or reading.** For example:

> "Now that we've heard this presentation on _____, take a minute to reflect on what you learned. Then, write one sentence—and only one, please—that summarizes what you'll be taking away from our meeting today."

2 **Participants reflect and summarize for 3 to 4 minutes.**

3 **Ask participants to take turns sharing their summaries.** Or ask them to pass their summaries to you to read aloud anonymously.

4 **Clarify any misunderstandings and conclude the meeting.**

➤ Use this structure as a way to check in with participants throughout a meeting. At various stopping points, ask them for a one-sentence summary to quickly get a sense of the group's understanding.

➤ Invite participants to work with a partner or small group and create a one-sentence summary that reflects their joint learning.

➤ Instead of a one-sentence summary, ask participants to give a one-word summary.

Learning Structure in Action

Clarifying Referral Procedures

At a staff meeting, the principal and head counselor presented clarifying information about the rationale behind the protocols guiding student referrals for disciplinary, academic, and other reasons. Participants were then asked to work in small groups to come up with a one-sentence summary that would give the presenters a quick sense of each group's understanding of the rationale.

The one-sentence summaries that volunteers shared with the whole group revealed one point of confusion that the presenters quickly cleared up before moving on to final questions and a brief concluding discussion.

One Word Around

IN BRIEF: A fast-paced word-association activity that can be used when introducing a new initiative or program. Gives a quick sense of people's thoughts and attitudes and helps shape a group discussion.

HOW TO DO IT

1 **Before the meeting, prepare three to five topics** for participants to focus on. For example, if you're introducing them to a new discipline approach, your topics might be "classroom rules," "teaching expectations," and "teacher language."

2 **Briefly introduce the activity.** For example:

> "I'll name a topic and then we'll go around the room. When it's your turn, say a word that quickly comes to mind. For instance, I might say 'rules' and you might say 'inconsistent' or 'playground.' I'll list your words and we'll use that to shape our bigger discussion. It's also perfectly OK to pass if you wish."

3 **Name the first topic for participants to consider.** Give a minute of think time if you feel it's needed. Go around the group and list the words people share. Repeat for your next topic.

4 **As a whole group, briefly reflect on what the list reveals** about people's thoughts and attitudes on each topic. Use this reflection as a springboard for further discussion.

Learning Structure in Action

Evolving Attitudes Toward Project-Based Learning

The district's curriculum coordinator has formed a Project-Based Learning (PBL) working group made up of representatives from each elementary school. For their first meeting, the coordinator shares background information about PBL and then uses One Word Around to get a quick sense of the group's attitudes about it.

After the group discusses the district's goals for PBL, the coordinator wraps up the meeting with another One Word Around. Together, the working group reflects on the differences between the two lists. The coordinator plans to use these lists and the group's discussion to create the agenda for the next meeting and ultimately to inform the district as it plans its PBL implementation.

Plusses and Challenges

IN BRIEF: Using a T-chart, participants brainstorm what's helping and hindering progress toward a goal, or strengths and weaknesses in implementation of a school initiative. Gives everyone a clear picture of what's working and what isn't and helps the team decide on next steps.

HOW TO DO IT

1 **Make an enlarged copy of the T-chart on page 82 and display it.** List the topic under discussion at the top of the chart (for example, "Safe and Calm Hallways").

2 **Remind participants of general guidelines for brainstorming:**

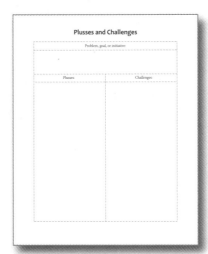

> ➤ The task is simply to generate a list of ideas, not to evaluate or judge them. There are no right or wrong ideas.

> ➤ Everyone will have a chance to offer ideas. Anyone may pass.

> ➤ Save any comments or questions for later. One exception: Asking clarifying questions is OK.

> ➤ Silence is OK. Pauses allow participants to think of new ideas or be more willing to share them.

3 **Invite participants to brainstorm the following:**

> ➤ **Plusses**—practices and structures that are helping progress toward the goal (for example, adults are teaching children how to walk quietly in hallways)

> ➤ **Challenges**—practices and structures that are missing or are hindering progress (for example, adults are not monitoring the hallways consistently)

CONTINUED

4 **Go around the room, giving everyone an initial turn to speak.** List participants' ideas on the chart. Then allow free-flowing brainstorming for as long as ideas continue to be generated, but not so long that participants disengage. The limit is usually 10 to 12 minutes.

5 **Open the floor** for about 5 minutes of comments and questions.

6 **As a whole group, address one or two challenges** and discuss possible next steps. Save the original list for future meetings in case you need to revisit the entire range of ideas generated.

─────────────────── **VARIATION** ───────────────────

➤ Do this activity in small groups. After groups complete their brainstorming, everyone reviews the other groups' lists before coming together as a whole group to complete Steps 5 and 6.

Learning Structure in Action

Improving Bus Behavior

By October, the principal has received numerous reports of misbehavior on busses. During a meeting with bus drivers and bus monitors, he uses Plusses and Challenges to generate a list of practices and structures that seem to be helping children behave positively (the plusses)

and a list of practices and structures that seem to be contributing to children's misbehavior (the challenges).

After discussing both lists, everyone agrees that they need to address two challenges: 1) reteaching children bus procedures and expectations and 2) ensuring that enough bus monitors are on duty for arrival and dismissal times.

Quick Text Analysis

IN BRIEF: Helps focus a discussion on the key concepts of an important article or report. Enables the facilitator to gauge what participants find most significant and use that information to guide the discussion.

HOW TO DO IT

1 **Give each participant a copy of the article or report to read.** If the piece is more than a few pages long, do this in advance.

2 **Introduce the activity.** For example:

> "I found this great article on high-quality math instruction. After you read it, highlight one word, one phrase, and one sentence that you found particularly meaningful. We'll use these highlights for our discussion."

3 **Allow enough time for everyone to read and highlight.**

4 **Going around the room, invite everyone to share their one highlighted sentence.** List these. Repeat for the one phrase and then for the one word. Encourage participants to hold their comments and questions until Step 5.

5 **Open up the discussion by asking participants to share what they notice about the sentences.** Do the same for the phrases and then the words. Or, if you need to wrap things up quickly, make a summary statement.

Learning Structure in Action

Guidelines for Inquiry-Based Science Instruction

After adopting a new science curriculum, the district's science coordinators hold a meeting with the science teachers to develop a common understanding of inquiry-based science instruction.

The coordinators pass out an article that reflects their thinking on using an inquiry-based approach in all grades. Then they use Quick Text Analysis to help teachers focus on key benefits of the approach and to begin the process of developing guidelines for using it throughout the district's elementary schools.

Quiz Trade

IN BRIEF: A quick, engaging way for participants to realize how much they've learned about a topic. It's also a way for discussion leaders to gauge participants' learning.

HOW TO DO IT

1 **Introduce the activity.** For example:

> "Now that we've heard this presentation on using a workshop model to teach language arts, we're going to quiz each other in a fun, low-pressure way on what we know about this model. This will help us all review the information and realize how much we've learned."

2 **Give each participant three index cards.** Ask participants to think about the most important points they got out of the presentation. On each card, participants write one question and answer that captures an important point (question on the front, answer on the back). Allow about 5 minutes for this step.

3 **Participants pair up.** Partner A reads one of her questions, and the pair share how they would each answer it, helping each other reach a deeper or more nuanced understanding of the issue. Then they switch roles, with Partner B reading one of his questions. Allow 5 minutes of discussion for each question, signaling when it's time to switch roles.

4 **Partners swap the cards that they discussed** and find new partners.

5 **In their new partnerships, partner A reads another of her original questions.** As in Step 3, the pair discusses how they would answer it. Then Partner B reads one of his original questions, they discuss, and swap those cards.

CONTINUED

6 **Repeat for a third round with new partners.** After these three rounds, each person will have traded their three cards for three new ones. They can use these new cards independently anytime for further reflection on the topic.

7 **Bring everyone together.** Ask volunteers to share one highlight from their discussions.

Learning Structure in Action

Reflecting on a Bullying Prevention Article

As part of a school's ongoing bullying prevention efforts, a counselor shows staff a video that reflects the school's efforts and provides additional strategies and tips. She uses Quiz Trade to help staff reflect on and share what they learned from the video.

Here are some of the participants' questions:

➤ "Why should we focus on the small stuff?"

➤ "How do we make sense of what we're seeing and hearing?"

➤ "What should we do if we notice unkind words or actions?"

Later on, after the meeting, the counselor sends out a follow-up email to the staff, thanking them for their engaged participation and summing up the highlights of their learning together.

Roam, Read, Retrieve

IN BRIEF: Participants visit various locations in the school to see what ideas they have for improving procedures for each location and then share those ideas. Gets participants up and moving, and allows everyone to hear multiple perspectives when developing or revising procedures.

HOW TO DO IT

1 **In advance, decide on three to five locations around the school** where better procedures are needed. Alternatively, decide on locations within one area, such as spots on the playground.

2 **Provide copies of the Roam, Read, Retrieve handout on page 83.** Then introduce the activity. For example:

> "We'll be visiting our reconfigured playground. At each of the marked spots, review the old procedures I've posted there. Then, on the handout, write down what changes you think are needed to ensure students' safety at each spot. You can work with a partner or in a small group if you'd like. Afterward, we'll discuss these ideas and start developing a new set of playground procedures."

3 **To keep things moving, suggest that participants spend only a minute or two at each location.** Give them a 30-second warning before you want them to regather as a whole group (or set a return time in advance).

4 **Use the completed handouts to prompt a whole-group discussion** or to guide your work in planning or revising procedures.

➤ You can also use this structure within a single room to reflect on project work, articles read, or videos watched. Small groups list responses to questions you pose or summarize their work on a piece of chart paper and then post their chart. Each group then uses Roam, Read, Retrieve to reflect on the other groups' work.

Learning Structure in Action

Rules and Routines for Common Areas

Near the end of the school year, the leadership team wants to review the rules and routines for entering and exiting three common areas—the gym, cafeteria, and library—to see if any changes are needed for next year. They use Roam, Read, Retrieve as part of a staff meeting.

To expedite this task, the team provides handouts that include the current rules and routines and asks staff to add their comments, questions, and suggestions to these handouts as they visit each location during the first half of the staff meeting. For the second half of the meeting, everyone comes back together to discuss possible revisions to the rules and routines for these three common areas.

Say Something

IN BRIEF: Participants analyze a reading or video clip with a partner or small group by stopping at designated points to make a comment or ask a question.

HOW TO DO IT

1. **Whether you're using a text or video clip, choose in advance the stopping points** at which participants will pause and make a brief comment or ask a question. For example, stopping points might be after every two paragraphs or at natural pauses during a video.

2. **Organize participants into pairs or small groups.** Have them read the text or watch the video.

3. **At each stopping point, participants take turns** in their partnerships or small groups, making a comment or asking a question. You may want to ask volunteers to take notes.

4. **Encourage participants to come up with their own unique comment or question,** rather than responding to what others say or ask. Tell them they'll have a chance to respond to others at the conclusion of the reading or video.

5. **After finishing the entire text or video clip, open a whole-group discussion.** Participants now share their reactions and respond to one another's questions and comments. (Reread or replay any sections they found confusing or worth emphasizing.)

➤ Allow each pair or group to determine their own stopping points so they move along at their own pace. (If using a video, each pair or group must be able to watch the video independent of the other pairs/groups.)

Learning Structure in Action

Understanding Child Development

As part of her efforts to help staff better understand the children they serve, the principal plans to strengthen the staff's knowledge of child development. She sets up separate meetings for staff at each grade level and uses Say Something to have them discuss the child development chapter of a recently published book.

Based on these grade-level discussions about child development, she creates a working group to develop a set of common goals and strategies for further increasing the staff's understanding of child development and creating a more child-centered learning environment.

Scavenger Hunt

IN BRIEF: Participants do a "scavenger hunt" for key information in a manual, website, or other resource as a way to engage with it. Especially useful for helping participants focus on particular points you deem critical to their roles and responsibilities.

HOW TO DO IT

1 **In advance, decide on five to ten items you want participants to look for** in the resource you're introducing to them. Write these on the Scavenger Hunt checklist on page 84.

2 **Make copies of the checklist and give one to each participant,** along with a copy of the resource.

3 **Introduce the activity.** For example:

> "Each of you has our updated policy manual and a scavenger hunt checklist. Let's take about 10 minutes to page through the manual and complete this checklist, which highlights the key changes. Then we'll go over the checklist together."

Remind participants to list the page number (or location) where they found the information.

4 **Allow just 10 to 15 minutes to complete the checklist** so that everyone stays engaged. If participants finish early, invite them to talk about their responses with someone else who's finished.

5 **Use the completed checklists to prompt a whole-group discussion.** Talk about each point on the checklist in order.

VARIATIONS

➤ Have participants complete their Scavenger Hunt checklists with a partner.

➤ Have participants complete their checklists before the meeting if you think you'll need all of the meeting time to go over the points.

Learning Structure in Action

Learning the School Safety Plan

To ensure that all staff is fully aware of the school's safety plan, the principal uses a scavenger hunt checklist to start the meeting. He passes out the policy manual and a checklist he created in collaboration with the district's other elementary school principals.

He then invites participants to work individually or with a partner to preview the manual and complete the checklist. Once everyone has completed their checklist, the principal goes over each item point by point, responds to any questions, and clarifies any confusion.

Snowball

IN BRIEF: A relaxed way to reflect on a topic from a previous meeting, learn others' perspectives, or wrap up a presentation or discussion. Can also be used to begin a meeting and generate first thoughts or questions about a topic.

HOW TO DO IT

1 **Introduce the activity.** For example:

> "For the last 10 minutes of our discussion on Common Core–aligned assessments, we'll each share anonymously one important piece of advice, question we have, or action we hope to take."

2 **Give each participant a slip of paper on which to write their advice, question, or action step.** Because this activity works best when it moves quickly, encourage participants to write down their first thought. Remind them not to write their name on the paper.

3 **On your signal, participants crumple up their paper (making a snowball) and drop it into a bag.** Pass the bag around the room and invite everyone to take one snowball. Or simply have participants toss their snowball on the floor and pick up one closest to them.

4 **Everyone takes turns reading aloud the snowball they chose.** You might want to list common ideas or themes on chart paper and hold a brief open discussion, prompting reflection with questions such as "What themes did you hear?" and "What stood out to you as you listened to your colleagues?"

➤ Once the snowballs are collected, have a volunteer toss one to each participant to catch and then read aloud.

➤ At Step 4, participants write a thoughtful response to the snowball they read aloud, crumple up the paper again, and repeat the activity.

Learning Structure in Action

Effective Lesson Design

A principal has been leading discussions with each grade level's teachers about effective parent conferences. She brings the whole teaching staff together to talk about common themes that came out of those discussions.

She then uses Snowball to wrap up this bigger discussion by inviting the group to respond to this question:

➤ "What piece of advice would you give your colleagues to consider when planning effective parent conferences?"

As participants read the ideas written on the snowballs they've chosen, a volunteer lists them. Later, the principal organizes and expands on these ideas and puts them up on the teacher page of the school's website for future reference.

Standing Vote

IN BRIEF: Participants cast their votes on an issue by standing up. Can be used any time discussion leaders want to quickly assess participants' views while simultaneously giving them a brief movement break.

HOW TO DO IT

1 **To see where people "stand" on an issue,** present them with one or more simple questions or statements.

2 **Invite participants to stand if they agree with the statement.** For example:

> "If you think we need to reteach our dismissal routines, please stand."

[pause for counting]

> "If you think we need to add hallway supervisors, please stand."

[pause for counting]

3 **Use the voting results to decide what to discuss next** or what steps to take as a group.

Learning Structure in Action

Assessing Parental Involvement

A school had identified improving school-home partnerships as a priority, so during the first few weeks of school, the principal wants to get a quick sense of parental communication with teachers.

At a staff meeting, he uses Standing Vote, asking staff to stand if parents have asked them questions or made comments to them about:

➤ Rules and discipline

➤ Curriculum and learning goals

➤ Social interactions

➤ Common areas (playground, cafeteria, bus, hallways)

➤ Homework

The principal then forms a staff committee, which uses information from this Standing Vote (along with a home survey sent out previously) to guide their exploration of how to improve school-home communications.

Step-by-Step

IN BRIEF: The facilitator quickly demonstrates a specific procedure and immediately gives participants a short, hands-on practice so everyone has a clear mental picture of how to carry it out. Best for procedures that staff will likely find challenging and ones that, for efficiency or safety, need to be done in a certain way.

HOW TO DO IT

1 **Introduce what you'll be demonstrating and briefly say why.** For example:

> "I'm going to show you the procedure for entering student data into our system. Following this procedure will save you time and make sure all our data is entered in a consistent way so that we can quickly retrieve information when we need it."

2 **Silently demonstrate the procedure exactly the way you want participants to do it.** As you demonstrate, avoid explaining what you are doing or why; rather, just show the steps so that participants' attention is on the steps, not on your voice. Keep your demonstration short.

3 **Invite participants to share what they noticed about your demonstration.** If necessary, prompt them to remember key aspects that you want to make sure everyone "gets." For example: "Before I went to the second screen, what did I do?"

4 **Have all participants practice exactly the way you showed them.**

5 **Provide feedback and coaching while participants practice.** To clarify any confusion, you may want to repeat your whole demonstration or just certain steps.

➤ To ensure that your demonstration goes smoothly, you may want to do a quick run-through with a colleague before the meeting.

➤ At Step 4, have a few people at a time practice, instead of people individually practicing, if equipment or time is limited.

Learning Structure in Action

Learning a New Data System

This year, a school district has been using a new software program to enter revised student and family information whenever a student moves into or out of the district. But mistakes are happening because many people are skipping some of the steps required to enter the data correctly and completely. As a result, families are not receiving needed information and staff must spend extra time directly contacting families and correcting the mistakes.

The district technology coordinator uses Step-by-Step to show the staff at each school the best way to enter new data. She also gives them all a chance to practice while giving them helpful feedback. As a result, mistakes are greatly reduced, staff have more time for other priorities, and families are getting the information they need on time.

Swap Meet

IN BRIEF: Participants form pairs, exchange one idea on a topic they've already been learning about, and then form new pairs. Useful for reflecting on a topic from a previous meeting, wrapping up a presentation or discussion, and ensuring that participants hear ideas from many different people.

HOW TO DO IT

1 **Pose a question for the group to consider and introduce the activity.** For example:

> "We're going to talk briefly with different partners as a follow-up to our discussion from last week on the new math curriculum. Here's the question to discuss: What do you feel is the strongest reason for changing our approach to teaching math, and why?"

2 **Give participants 1 to 2 minutes to think of their response to the question.**

3 **Participants find a partner and quickly swap responses.** They then find new partners and keep repeating this process. Encourage participants to collect as many ideas as possible, but at least three.

4 **After 5 to 7 minutes, signal for the swapping to end.**

5 **Bring everyone back together.** Ask volunteers to share one idea they collected.

VARIATION

➤ Have participants write down their response before they start swapping with partners, and then add each new idea they collect to their paper. They can use their collection of ideas later to reflect further on the topic.

Learning Structure in Action

Giving Students More Academic Choices

A school's math coach is working with grade-level teachers on ways to incorporate more student choices for learning into their math lessons. The coach believes having more choices will help motivate and engage students in their learning.

To wrap up a departmental meeting on this topic, the coach uses Swap Meet so participants can gather ideas from as many colleagues as possible. When participants have finished swapping ideas, the coach invites them to each contribute one or two ideas to a list on the white-board, which he then prints out for everyone to have as a takeaway.

Think, Pair, Share

IN BRIEF: Participants have a short, focused conversation with a partner and then summarize for the whole group. Allows group leaders to get a sense of participants' thoughts and questions about a topic. Can be used throughout a presentation to give participants multiple chances to interact with a partner.

HOW TO DO IT

1 **In advance, prepare up to three topics or questions for participants to discuss.** An example of a question might be:

> "What can we do to give students more practice in listening skills throughout the day?"

2 **Briefly introduce the activity.** For example:

> "Today we're going to learn more about the speaking and listening skills in the Common Core State Standards. To kick off our session, I'm going to pose a question. You'll pair up to discuss it, and then each pair will share one or two key points from their discussion."

3 **Pose your first question.** Give a minute or so of think time. You may want to play some soothing music during this time.

4 **Everyone pairs up with a neighbor to discuss their thoughts.** (Assign partners in advance if you'd like.) Allow a few minutes for this discussion. Repeat this step if you want pairs to discuss more than one question or topic.

CONTINUED

5 **Pairs raise their hands when they're ready to share one or two key ideas with the whole group.** When most hands are up, give the rest of the group about 30 more seconds to wrap up their conversations.

6 **Invite one person from each pair to share.** You may also want to invite participants to write out and post their key ideas.

VARIATION

➤ Do this as a Think, Write, Pair, Share. In Step 3, have participants write down their thoughts before they share with a partner.

Learning Structure in Action

Working With Parents

In response to the results from a parent survey, the principal wants all teachers to make a concerted effort to involve parents with their child's learning. To start this work on a positive note, the principal invites everyone at a staff meeting to respond to the following question, using Think, Pair, Share:

➤ "What are the main ways you work with parents to engage them in their child's learning?"

After each pair has shared one or two key ideas from their discussion, the principal begins his presentation and exploration of effective ways to engage parents in their child's education. In his presentation, he makes sure to connect his information to their ideas.

Three, Two, One

IN BRIEF: Participants write down a few brief thoughts to check their understanding of a topic. Useful for prompting a discussion or reviewing previous learning. Also allows facilitators to quickly assess learning and interest.

HOW TO DO IT

1 **Give each participant a copy of the Three, Two, One form on page 85.** Then explain what they need to do:

> ➤ List three big ideas that you learned today.

> ➤ List two questions that you have—for example, do you need a point clarified or want to learn more about a topic?

> ➤ List one takeaway, or practical tip, that you plan to try.

2 **Use the completed forms for a brief, concluding discussion.** You could invite each participant to share one idea with the whole group. You may also want to collect the forms and use them to plan the next meeting or training.

➤ Use Three, Two, One at a few stopping points throughout the meeting. This helps participants continuously assess their learning and allows you to check their understanding and interest along the way.

➤ Change the categories for each number. For example, ask participants to list three questions, two suggestions, and one big idea or takeaway. Or adapt the structure for a compare-and-contrast exercise: three similarities, two differences, one question or takeaway.

Learning Structure in Action

Tips for a Successful Back-to-School Night

At a staff meeting to plan for back-to-school night, the principal shares a few insights and tips for successful presentations to parents. He asks the staff to reflect on what he's shared and connect it to their individual planning for back-to-school night.

Then he passes out a Three, Two, One form for them to complete and uses it to prompt a broader discussion of the school's key goals for communicating and connecting with parents at this event and throughout the school year.

Two True, One False

IN BRIEF: An engaging way to reinforce essential information and dispel any myths or points of confusion. This structure is also useful for prompting participants to carefully read a text that they'll later discuss together.

HOW TO DO IT

1 **Give each participant a copy of the Two True, One False form on page 86.** Then introduce the activity. For example:

> "Now that we've all read _____, let's see what we've learned from it. After you complete the form, we'll go around and check to see if we all have the same understanding."

2 **Give participants enough time to complete the reading** (or have them read before the meeting). Allow about 5 minutes for filling out the form. If necessary, explain how to use the form:

➤ Write two statements that you think accurately reflect two key points from the reading.

➤ Write one statement that is false or reflects a common misunderstanding.

3 **Invite a volunteer to read their statements aloud,** but in random order and without labeling them as true or false.

CONTINUED

4 **Discuss the statements as a group.** The goal is to identify the true statements and the false one and to provide explanations for why, using the reading and other relevant information as evidence.

5 **Repeat with additional volunteers reading their statements** as time allows.

Learning Structure in Action

Clarifying RTI and IEP Processes

At a staff meeting, the heads of academic counseling and special education review the procedures and protocols for RTI (Response to Intervention) and IEPs (Individualized Education Plans). These leaders ask everyone to read a document they compiled that provides step-by-step processes for working with RTI and IEPs.

For each process, they invite participants to complete a Two True, One False handout and then discuss a few responses as a whole group. At the conclusion of this meeting, the two leaders decide to use the staff's feedback to clarify their descriptions of the procedures and protocols and make their document easier to use.

Walk and Talk

IN BRIEF: As participants walk with a partner, they discuss a given topic or question. Gets participants moving, which can help spark deeper thinking, especially when group energy is low.

HOW TO DO IT

1 **State the topic or question for participants to discuss in pairs.** For example:

> "As you stroll the building, discuss what we can do to improve transitions in the hallways."

> "Walk with a partner and talk about your plans for getting the second half of the year off to a strong start. Think about students' academic and social-emotional competencies."

Encourage participants to Walk and Talk with someone they don't usually work with or know that well.

2 **Suggest that participants jot down notes** or record their conversation on a smartphone or tablet as they walk.

3 **Allow 5 to 10 minutes for the Walk and Talk.** Provide a 1-minute warning signal or set a time for the whole group to regather.

4 **Bring the group back together and ask each pair to report one or two ideas** or to summarize their discussion.

➤ Combine with Three, Two, One (page 66) or Two True, One False (page 68):
Have pairs walk as they generate ideas together for completing the forms for
those activities.

Learning Structure in Action

Reducing Student Tardiness

Although daily attendance is consistently high,
a school's social worker (who is charged with
monitoring attendance) notices a high rate of
tardiness. She's also hearing from teachers of
how this tardiness is negatively impacting students' learning and the classroom community.

Before the next staff meeting, she provides everyone with
an attendance and tardiness report. At the meeting, she
quickly summarizes the report and provides an update.
Then she uses Walk and Talk, prompting the staff to stroll
the halls as they think of reasons for the high levels of tardiness and possible solutions to try.

After the Walk and Talk, she invites each pair to summarize their discussions. They consolidate their ideas and
agree on a set of strategies to try.

Walk Around Survey

IN BRIEF: A blank three-by-three grid prompts participants to review and reflect on their learning with their colleagues. The completed grids can also serve as a quick assessment of participants' learning.

HOW TO DO IT

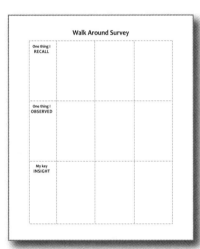

1 **Give each participant a copy of the three-by-three grid on page 87.**

2 **Introduce the activity.** For example:

> "Before we continue our discussion about revising the student handbook, we're going to do a Walk Around Survey. This will help us reflect on last week's discussion and guide today's work. Your goal is to get nine colleagues to complete your grid, one colleague's idea per box."

It's OK if what a colleague writes in a box repeats what someone else wrote.

3 **Invite participants to find a partner and exchange grids.** They each fill in one box, initial it, and give the grids back.

4 **Use an auditory signal every minute or so to prompt participants to find a new partner** and keep the exchange of ideas flowing. Participants continue mixing and mingling until all nine boxes of their grids are completed.

5 **As time allows, ask for volunteers to share with the whole group** one item from their grid.

VARIATION

➤ To stretch the group's reflections, challenge them not to repeat what a colleague has already written on a grid.

Learning Structure in Action

Building Working Memory in Students

A school psychologist gives a presentation to the staff about working memory and how it can impact a child's learning. She also provides techniques and resources for working directly with children to build their working memory.

Because this is a new topic for most of the staff, the school psychologist concludes her talk by having everyone do a Walk Around Survey. Then she has everyone share one key idea from their completed grids. Hearing their thoughts helps her assess their understanding of working memory and correct any misconceptions. Participants leave the meeting with ideas they can begin using right away.

World Café

IN BRIEF: Participants move in and out of ongoing, small-group conversations. This free-flowing, but still structured, format enables participants to hear multiple perspectives on various topics they're learning about.

HOW TO DO IT

1 **Arrange the room café-style by spreading out tables and chairs** (four to five chairs per table). Invite participants to sit at the table of their choice.

2 **Give each table a discussion topic related to the issue they're learning about.** For example, if they're learning about teacher language, topic A might be reinforcing language, topic B reminding language, and so on. It's OK to repeat topics.

3 **Provide a question to focus participants' discussion.** For example, "What comes easily and doesn't come easily for you when you try to use this type of language?" Allow about 5 minutes for discussion.

4 **Give a signal to wrap up conversations** and invite two or three people per table to change tables.

5 **Pose a new focusing question or use the same one.** Everyone discusses it with their new tablemates. Do several more rounds of table changes as time allows.

6 **Bring the group back together** and invite one person from each table to share out.

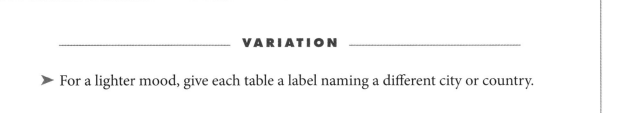

VARIATION

➤ For a lighter mood, give each table a label naming a different city or country.

Learning Structure in Action

Building Belonging, Significance, and Engagement

A principal is seeking ideas for how to get students more invested in school and strengthen the learning community. As she meets with various staff groups, she uses World Café to elicit their ideas.

The principal assigns each table one of three topics—Belonging, Significance, Engagement—and has participants talk about their ideas for promoting students' sense of these on a schoolwide basis. She then synthesizes the ideas she hears from the various groups and shares them with everyone at a whole-staff meeting.

Written Conversations

IN BRIEF: Participants build on one another's ideas by writing a response to a question or topic you pose and then exchanging papers. Useful when participants would benefit from a quiet, thoughtful reflection time.

HOW TO DO IT

1 **Arrange the room so participants can sit in small groups of four to six.** Encourage participants to sit with people they don't usually work with or know that well.

2 **State a topic or pose a question.** Give participants time to think and free-write, but keep this time relatively brief (2 to 3 minutes).

3 **Give participants a 30-second warning to finish up their writing.**

4 **Participants pass their papers to the right.** Then they read and respond to their colleague's writing or add to it. Again, keep this step relatively short and provide a warning signal.

5 **Repeat this process until each paper returns to its original writer or as time allows.** Invite participants to share interesting comments or summarize what was written in their small group for the whole group.

Learning Structure in Action

Starting and Ending the Day More Powerfully

During December, the principal notices teachers slipping in their use of Morning Meeting to begin the day and closing circles to end it. He also notices that teachers and students both seem to be struggling to stay engaged this month. During a staff meeting, he describes for teachers what he's noticing and then uses Written Conversations to have staff respond to this question:

"How can we better use Morning Meetings and closing circles as bookends to boost students' engagement in learning and our own engagement with teaching?"

After participants have shared their ideas, they discuss next steps that will help them improve their use of Morning Meetings and closing circles.

HANDOUTS

Geometric Forms

☐   Something I learned that "squares" with my thinking

◯   A question that is still "circling" in my mind

△   Three important "points" I want to remember

⇒   One new "direction" I will go in (or action I will take)

1)

2)

3)

Note-Taking

Topic: _____

_____

_____

_____

_____

_____

Topic: _____

_____

_____

_____

_____

_____

Topic: _____

_____

_____

_____

_____

_____

Plusses and Challenges

Problem, goal, or initiative:

Plusses:	Challenges:

Roam, Read, Retrieve

1st Location: _____

   Questions, comments, or suggestions:

➤ _____

➤ _____

➤ _____

2nd Location: _____

   Questions, comments, or suggestions:

➤ _____

➤ _____

➤ _____

3rd Location: _____

   Questions, comments, or suggestions:

➤ _____

➤ _____

➤ _____

Scavenger Hunt

1. Look for: _____

Page number or location where found: _____

2. Look for: _____

Page number or location where found: _____

3. Look for: _____

Page number or location where found: _____

4. Look for: _____

Page number or location where found: _____

5. Look for: _____

Page number or location where found: _____

6. Look for: _____

Page number or location where found: _____

7. Look for: _____

Page number or location where found: _____

8. Look for: _____

Page number or location where found: _____

9. Look for: _____

Page number or location where found: _____

10. Look for: _____

Page number or location where found: _____

Three, Two, One

Three Big Ideas:

➤ _____

_____

➤ _____

_____

➤ _____

_____

Two Questions:

➤ _____

_____

➤ _____

_____

One Takeaway:

➤ _____

_____

Two True, One False

Two True:

➤ _____

_____

_____

_____

➤ _____

_____

_____

_____

One False:

➤ _____

_____

_____

_____

Walk Around Survey

One thing I RECALL			
One thing I OBSERVED			
My key INSIGHT			

The Morning Meeting Book, 3rd edition

A well-structured Morning Meeting warms students up for a day of engaged learning while building community and giving students a chance to practice social and academic skills. The new 3rd edition includes all the material that has made this comprehensive, user-friendly book a teacher favorite along with new activities, updated examples, and connections to Common Core standards and social-emotional competencies.

Roxann Kriete, Carol Davis • 232 pp. • K–8
ISBN 978-1-892989-60-4 • $24

The Power of Our Words: Teacher Language That Helps Children Learn, 2nd edition

Learn how to use words, tone, and pacing to build a classroom where students feel safe, respected, and excited about learning. Practical information, concise explanations, concrete examples, and quick-scan charts help build proficiency in the skillful use of positive teacher language.

Paula Denton • 192 pp. • K–6
ISBN 978-1-892989-59-8 • $24

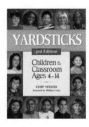

Yardsticks: Children in the Classroom Ages 4–14, 3rd edition

Use developmental knowledge to boost academic and social learning. Clear, concise narrative and easy-to-scan charts summarize children's physical, social, emotional, language, and cognitive growth patterns, needs, and strengths at each age.

Chip Wood • 240 pp. • K–8
ISBN 978-1-892989-19-2 • $22 (paper)
ISBN 978-1-892989-21-5 • $30 (hardcover)

The First Six Weeks of School

Build a solid foundation for classroom life during the first six weeks of school. The result: increased student motivation, cooperation, responsibility, and self-management. Detailed plans, guidelines, and resource lists.

Paula Denton, Roxann Kriete • 240 pp. • K–6
ISBN 978-1-892989-04-8 • $24

The Language of Learning: Teaching Students Core Thinking, Listening, and Speaking Skills

Teach the essential communication skills that every child needs for developing into a highly engaged, self-motivated learner. This guide offers practical approaches to teaching students how to listen and understand, think before speaking, ask thoughtful questions and give high-quality answers, agree thoughtfully and disagree respectfully, and more!

Margaret Berry Wilson • 216 pp. • K–6
ISBN 978-1-892989-61-1 • $24

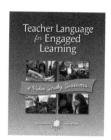

Teacher Language for Engaged Learning: 4 Video Study Sessions

Learn communication strategies that highly effective teachers use to support students' high-level thinking, active participation, and collaboration. This kit includes step-by-step guidelines and all materials needed for leading 30-minute professional development sessions, each built around a 10-minute video segment, on four topics: Asking Open-Ended Questions; Giving Clear Directions; Giving High-Quality Feedback; and Keeping the Focus on Learning.

Boxed kit with DVD
ISBN 978-1-892989-55-0 • $195

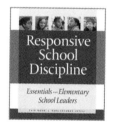

Responsive School Discipline: Essentials for Elementary School Leaders

Bring positive behavior to your school through strong, consistent, and positive discipline. Experienced administrators offer practical strategies for building a safe, calm, and respectful school climate—strategies based on deep respect for children and for staff. Each chapter targets one key discipline issue and starts with a check-list of action steps.

Chip Wood, Babs Freeman-Loftis • 272 pp. • K–6
ISBN 978-1-892989-43-7 • $24

Teasing, Tattling, Defiance and More: Positive Approaches to 10 Common Classroom Behaviors

Get better at handling behaviors that disrupt classrooms and interfere with learning. This practical guide includes an overview of the *Responsive Classroom* approach to discipline and simple, effective techniques for addressing problem behaviors, explaining which proactive strategies to use, how to respond most effectively when children misbehave, and how to talk with parents.

Margaret Berry Wilson • 272 pp. • K–6
ISBN 978-1-892989-54-3 • $24

ABOUT THE PUBLISHER

Northeast Foundation for Children, Inc., a not-for-profit educational organization, is the developer of *Responsive Classroom*®, an evidence-based approach to elementary education that is associated with greater teacher effectiveness, higher student achievement, and improved school climate. *Responsive Classroom* practices help educators develop competencies in three interrelated areas: engaging academics, positive community, and effective management. We offer the following resources for elementary school educators:

Professional Development Services

➤ Workshops for teachers and administrators (locations around the country and on-site)

➤ On-site consulting services to support implementation

➤ Resources for site-based study

➤ National conference for school and district leaders

Publications and Resources

➤ Books and videos for teachers and school leaders

➤ Professional development kits for school-based study

➤ Website with extensive library of free articles: www.responsiveclassroom.org

➤ Free newsletter for elementary educators

➤ The *Responsive*® blog, with news, ideas, and advice from and for elementary educators

For details, contact:

Northeast Foundation for Children, Inc.
85 Avenue A, P.O. Box 718
Turners Falls, Massachusetts 01376-0718

800-360-6332   www.responsiveclassroom.org
info@responsiveclassroom.org